A Peacemaker for Warring Nations

The Founding of the Iroquois League

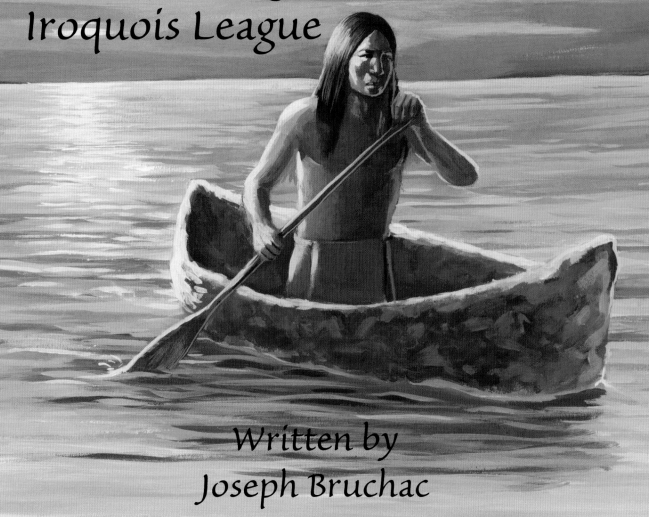

Written by
Joseph Bruchac

Illustrated by
David Kanietakeron Fadden

✦Wisdom Tales✦

A Peacemaker for Warring Nations: The Founding of the Iroquois League
Text © Joseph Bruchac 2021; Illustrations © David Kanietakeron Fadden 2021

Wisdom Tales in an imprint of World Wisdom, Inc.

Library of Congress Cataloging-in-Publication

Names: Bruchac, Joseph, 1942- author. | Fadden, David Kanietakeron,
illustrator.
Title: A Peacemaker for warring nations : the founding of the Iroquois
League / written by Joseph Bruchac ; illustrated by David Kanietakeron
Fadden.
Description: Bloomington : Wisdom Tales, [2021] | Includes bibliographical
references. | Audience: Ages 4-8 | Audience: Grades 2-3 | Summary: "The
League of the Iroquois was a true representational democracy-so much so
that the United States Constitution is said to have been modeled on some
of its tenets. But how, perhaps a thousand years before the time of
Columbus, did the Five Iroquois Nations (the Mohawk, Onondaga, Oneida,
Cayuga, and Seneca) come to end the bitter eye-for-eye warfare among
them? What brought them together in an alliance based on the Great Law
of Peace? And how was it that a system of Clan Mothers was instituted in
which women are seen as the center of the nation and still today choose
the 50 royaners, or peace chiefs, who speak for their respective
communities in meetings of the League? In A Peacemaker for Warring
Nations, renowned Native author Joseph Bruchac draws from the teachings
of both contemporary and past Iroquois tradition bearers in telling the
inspiring story of how "the Peacemaker," a divine messenger sent by the
Creator, helped to bring reconciliation to warring nations. The book is
beautifully and accurately illustrated by David Kanietakeron Fadden, a
respected Mohawk artist whose work honors his deep indigenous roots"--
Provided by publisher.
Identifiers: LCCN 2020035239 (print) | LCCN 2020035240 (ebook) | ISBN
9781937786878 (hardback) | ISBN 9781937786885 (epub)
Subjects: LCSH: Five Nations--History--Juvenile literature. | Iroquois
Indians--History--Juvenile literature. | Iroquois Indians--Folklore.
Classification: LCC E99.I7 B855 2021 (print) | LCC E99.I7 (ebook) | DDC
974.7004/9755--dc23
LC record available at https://lccn.loc.gov/2020035239
LC ebook record available at https://lccn.loc.gov/2020035240

Printed in China on acid-free paper.

For information address Wisdom Tales,
P.O. Box 2682, Bloomington, Indiana, 47402-2682
www.wisdomtalespress.com

PREFACE

Although I've done years of research in the many books written about the "Iroquois League," my knowledge of the Peacemaker's great confederacy owes just as much—if not more—to contemporary Haudenosaunee[1] tradition bearers. Sharing their oral traditions about the Peacemaker and the founding of the League of Five Nations (comprising the Mohawk, Onondaga, Oneida, Cayuga, and Seneca) is something that the Haudenosaunee have been doing for a thousand years. In the eighteenth century, Iroquois teachers brought such "Founding Fathers" of the American nation as Benjamin Franklin to meetings of the League to show them the importance of unifying their colonies in a similar fashion. Haudenosaunee people continue trying to teach European Americans—and the world—about the Great Law.

Two of those teachers—who I've been honored to know as friends, are the late Chief Jake Tekaronianekwen Swamp and Tom Sakokwenionkwas Porter. Jake formed his Tree of Peace Society in 1984 and traveled the world—often to conflict zones—to tell about the Peacemaker and plant symbolic trees of peace. In 1996 he released an audio tape of his telling of the Peacemaker's story called *The Peacemaker's Journey*.

One of the nine chiefs of the Akwesasne Mohawk Nation from 1971 to 1992, Tom left the reservation to create a new tradition-based community called Kanatsiohareke (Place of the Clean Pot) along the Mohawk River on traditional Mohawk land. There, Tom often does programs in which he tells the stories of the Peacemaker.

The telling of the Peacemaker's story in this book is strongly based on what I have learned over the years from those elders I've just mentioned and others.

—Joseph Bruchac

---

[1] I use the words "Iroquois" and "Haudenosaunee" interchangeably, even though the word "Iroquois" comes from the Abenaki language. Both words are acceptable and, in fact, the word "Iroquois" is more commonly used by Haudenosaunee people themselves. That is also true of the names of Seneca and Mohawk—both of which come from Algonquin languages. A book could easily be written about the many names now used to identify different Native nations which were not their own original names for themselves . . . one of the many still-existing legacies of colonialism.

Many centuries ago, before the Europeans came to this land on the back of the Great Turtle, there were five strong nations.

Once they had lived as sisters and brothers with similar languages and ways of life. They had all been given the same original instructions from Teharonhia:wako, the Creator—to treat all things with respect, to always give thanks for the many gifts of life.

But, somehow, they had forgotten. Now the five nations lived at war with each other and every other nation around them. No one remembered how the fighting began, but all felt its results. Whenever one nation was attacked, its warriors struck back with equal violence. If one of their people was killed, they would kill one of the enemy. No longer was anyone safe. It seemed it would never end.

Teharonhia:wako was troubled. Such taking of lives was not the way things were meant to be. A messenger had to be sent to bring back balance and peace.

To the north of the Five Nations was the Wendat Nation. There was fighting and turmoil among those people, too. A woman named End of the Field lived there with her daughter, She Walks Ahead. End of the Field decided to move with her child to a safer place where they could hide from any warriors. She took her to a place on the north shore of Kanontar:io, the beautiful lake, a place called Hill Where the Eagles Flew.

It was there that She Walks Ahead grew into womanhood. One day, her mother noticed her daughter's body was changing.

"My daughter," she said, "Have you been seeing someone?"

"No," She Walks Ahead replied. "I have seen no one. I do not understand why this is happening."

End of the Field became angry. Who was the father of the child her daughter was carrying? Why would her daughter not tell her?

Before long, She Walks Ahead gave birth to a strong and healthy boy.

End of the Field was certain that this child was bad. He would bring evil to their family. It was winter and the nearby river was covered with ice.

"I will take a walk with your child," she said. She walked out onto the river, cut a hole in the ice and thrust the boy into it. "We are rid of him now," she said to herself. But when she got back to their lodge she heard the sound of a baby laughing. She looked inside and saw the boy in her daughter's arms.

"Truly," End of the Field thought, "this is the child of an evil spirit."

The next day she said again that she would take the baby for a walk. This time she buried him deep in snow. But when she got back to the camp, once again the baby was there with his mother. So, on the third morning, she took the child far into the woods, made a big fire and thrust the child into it, watching him burn.

However, just as before, when she got back to their camp, the baby was there sleeping peacefully in his mother's arms.

That night, as End of the Field tried to sleep, she heard scratching at the door

"I have come from the West," the shadowy figure said. "Your daughter has done nothing wrong. You must stop trying to kill your grandchild. He was sent by the Creator to bring a message of peace. There is too much bloodshed in the world and his job will be to bring the people back together. His name will be Tekana:wita, Two Currents Coming Together, a name never to be used again for anyone else."

Then the shadowy figure walked away and disappeared.

The next day, when End of the Field looked outside their lodge, she saw footprints in the earth, like those of a giant hare.

She told her daughter about the messenger who had visited them. She promised to care for her and her grandson so that he could carry out his mission to be a messenger of peace.

Tekana:wita began to grow, much faster than a normal child. Soon he was a young man and End of the Field decided it was time for them to return to their people.

"I am glad," Two Currents said. "I have a message to bring to them."

The war chief was pleased to see them return.

"We feared you had been killed or taken captive by enemies," he said.

"We have returned," End of the Field said, "because my grandson has a message for you."

An assembly was called and Two Currents spoke to them about the right way to live, about the need to end their fighting, to live righteously and in peace.

Though young, his voice was calm and certain. The war chief and elders were moved by his words. They decided to try to follow this new way of peace.

In the days that followed, all the people listened as one they now called the Peacemaker taught them how to give thanks to the Creator. He taught them the sacred ceremonies that had been forgotten, the Feather Dance, the Drum Dance, the Personal Song.

The Peacemaker's job had just begun, though. He now had to undertake a great journey. He and his mother and grandmother returned to Hill Where the Eagles Flew. He began to build a canoe, carving it out of white stone.

"I am leaving," he said to his mother and grandmother. "I will not be returning."

Then he set out across Kanontar:io, the Beautiful Lake.

A man who was watching from the south side of the lake saw him approaching. That man was one who had always hoped that someone would come and bring peace to his people. His name was I Do Everything Right. When the Peacemaker reached the shore in his white canoe, I Do Everything Right saw that he had no weapons.

"Where are you from?" he asked.

"I am from the north," the Peacemaker replied. "There the people are now beginning to live in peace. Where are you from?"

"I have fled from a Kanien;keha village to escape warfare."

"I have come to end the killing," the Peacemaker replied. "Go home to your village and tell the people I will arrive soon to bring them a message."

"The people here are dangerous," I Do Everything Right said. "They will kill you."

The Peacemaker smiled. "Those are the ones I want to meet."

I Do Everything Right did as the Peacemaker asked. He made the journey back to his village and told the rarontaron, the war chief, that a man was coming with a message of peace.

The war chief laughed at him. "Why should we care about one man's foolish message? If he comes here, we will kill him."

The second war chief, though, felt differently. The idea of a message of peace moved him. He said nothing, but he waited eagerly for the man carrying that

Meanwhile, the Peacemaker went west to the land of the Kakwako, the Neutral Nation. There, along the war trail, lived the woman known as Jigonhsaseh, Round Face Like a Lynx. She had been given the job of feeding the warriors who passed her way, offering them council and settling their disputes. Anyone fleeing from enemies could seek shelter in her lodge.

"Who is chasing you?" she said to the Peacemaker.

"No one," the Peacemaker replied. "I have come here to bring a message of peace. When I end warfare, you will have a new role. You and the headwomen of the different clans will choose the leaders and they will abide by your will. We will build a Longhouse of One Family and its light will shine throughout the world. You will be the mother of all the nations when the Great Tree of Peace has been planted."

Jigonhsaseh heard the truth of his words. "It will be as you say," she said. "I embrace this message that you have brought."

"Now I must leave," the Peacemaker said. "But we will meet again when the nations of our family come together at Onondaga."

Then the Peacemaker traveled east for many days until he came to the eastern edge of the Kanien:keha people, to the place called Skanehtateh near the great Cohoes Falls. Here he would begin to build his Longhouse of One Family. The Kanien:keha, the Flint People, the Mohawk nation, would be the first rafter. He made camp on a hill looking over the falls and built a fire.

The next morning, the people of the nearby Mohawk village saw smoke rising from the direction of the river. Such smoke was the sign of someone who wished to approach their village. Runners were sent out. There, on the hill above the falls, sat a stranger smoking a pipe.

"I mean you no harm," he said. "Allow me to enter your village. I have come to bring an important message."

"Why should we listen to you?" the runners asked. "We can kill you now and eat your heart."

"Go tell your war chief I want to speak to him," the Peacemaker replied in a calm voice. "If he does not like my message, you can kill me."

Impressed by his bravery, the runners went back to their chief and told him what the strange man had said.

"Go and tell him he can enter our village," the rarontaron said. "This must be the one that I Always Do Right told us about. I want to hear his words."

When the Peacemaker arrived, the war chief and his two assistants listened to his message.

"The Creator is sad that warfare if everywhere. Good people are dying and their bones are everywhere on the earth. We should all have a good mind and live in harmony together with generosity and respect. You war chiefs must be the first to throw away your weapons. New leaders must be chosen to be peace chiefs. A peace chief will be known as a royaner, a Tree of Equal Height and never again take the path of war."

When the Peacemaker finished speaking, the head war chief stood.

"I like your message," he said, "but I do not think it will work."

"If you wish," the Peacemaker said, "You may test me to see if my message is true."

"Yes, let us test him," said the war chief's first assistant, the one who had been secretly waiting for the Peacemaker to arrive. "There is a tree by the great gorge with a branch hanging over the river. Let him sit on that branch and we will cut it off so that he falls into the gorge. If he was sent by the Creator he will survive."

"That is a good idea," the head war chief said, "Tell all our people to come and see what happens."

The next day, everyone gathered at the gorge. They watched as the Peacemaker climbed up and sat on the branch. With their stone axes, the warriors cut the branch and watched the Peacemaker plummet into the river far below and disappear in the rapids.

"It is settled," the war chief said. "That man is gone and will not return."

The next day, though, the smoke of a campfire was seen rising near the gorge. Runners were sent to see who it was. There, sitting by his fire, was the man who had fallen into the gorge. They approached him fearfully, but the Peacemaker smiled at them.

"Go back to your village," he said. "Prepare the people for my visit."

When the war chief heard that the man he had doubted was alive, he knew that the Peacemaker was indeed a messenger from the Creator. A special seat was prepared for him and he was welcomed warmly.

"I put down my title as rarontaron. We accept your message of peace," the war chief said. "Tell us more of what it means."

"Everyone now will be of a good mind," the Peacemaker explained. "When one accepts this way, others will follow. It will be like a ball in the snow, growing larger as it rolls forward."

Then the Peacemaker told the former war chief that he would now be a royaner. Because he was the first to put down his title, he would now be first on the roll of fifty chiefs. He would always abide by the will of the council of women. His job would be to represent, not rule his people. He and all those who took his place in the future, would be known as Tekarihokenh, He Was of Two Minds. The second war chief, who had hoped for the Peacemaker's success was also made a royaner.

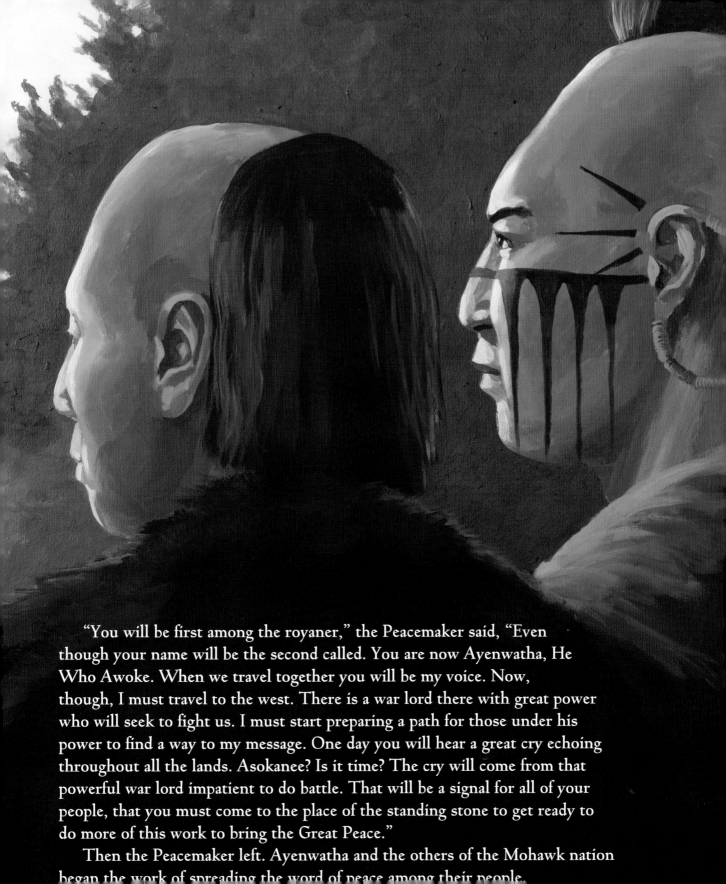

"You will be first among the royaner," the Peacemaker said, "Even though your name will be the second called. You are now Ayenwatha, He Who Awoke. When we travel together you will be my voice. Now, though, I must travel to the west. There is a war lord there with great power who will seek to fight us. I must start preparing a path for those under his power to find a way to my message. One day you will hear a great cry echoing throughout all the lands. Asokanee? Is it time? The cry will come from that powerful war lord impatient to do battle. That will be a signal for all of your people, that you must come to the place of the standing stone to get ready to do more of this work to bring the Great Peace."

Then the Peacemaker left. Ayenwatha and the others of the Mohawk nation began the work of spreading the word of peace among their people.

Although Ayenwatha had lost his wife years before, he still had three daughters he loved deeply. But as he worked to spread the word of peace, first one and then another of his daughters became ill. The medicine society tried to cure them, but nothing worked. Someone powerful had sent bad medicine against them and both died.

To ease Ayenwatha's grief, the people decided to play the sacred game of tewaraethon, lacrosse. But as they played, a great cry filled the heavens. Asokanee? Asokanee? Asokanee? Then a huge purple bird flew down over the crowd of lacrosse players, distracting them so much that they trampled Ayenwatha's third daughter, killing her.

The burden of his grief was so great that Ayenwatha could not bear to remain in his village. He began to wander toward the west, avoiding all human contact. How could it be that this happened after he did so much to help the people? His mind was confused and he felt lost.

Finally he came to a place where elderberry bushes loaded with fruit were growing and an idea came to him. He picked some of those berries and strung them onto slender peeled saplings, making 14 strings that looked much like wampum strings made of shells. Then he thrust two forked sticks in the ground and placed a single stick upon them to make a rack.

"If someone bore the burden of grief as I do," Ayenwatha said, "I would console them. I would wipe the tears from their eyes with a cloth made from the skin of a young fawn." Then he hung one of the strings over the stick.

A sound came from the bushes behind him and the Peacemaker stepped into the clearing, holding a fawn skin cloth. He picked up the wampum string and spoke in a kind voice.

"Ayenwatha, if anyone was as burdened by grief as you are, I would wipe the tears from their eyes with this fawn skin so they could again see clearly."

Then he wiped the tears from Ayenwatha's eyes and picked up another string. One by one, using one string after another, he spoke the words that would be known as the Condolence Ceremony, clearing Ayenwatha's ears so he could again hear the words of healing, clearing his throat so he could again speak words that were understood, lifting the darkness from his mind and spirit and telling him what must be done. When at last the Peacemaker was done, Ayenwatha spoke.

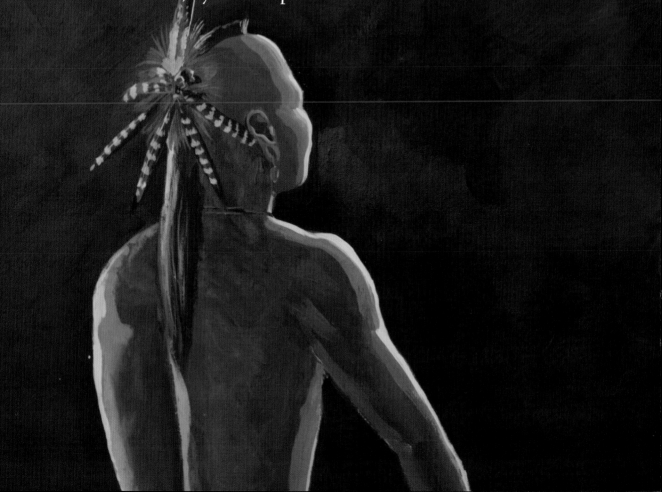

"I am better now. Truly we have found a way so that everyone may deal with their grief and continue onward."

The Peacemaker nodded. "Now that we have found this way to comfort the nations, we must continue to make a path. Go to the Wolf Clan village of the Oneota:keha, the People of the Standing Stone. In a few days I will meet you there."

At the Oneida village, Ayenwatha was escorted to the rarontaron of the wolf clan. Using an eagle feather he had cut into three pieces, he taught the war chief the first three parts of the Condolence address. Handing him each piece in turn, Ayenwatha spoke the words of wiping the tears of grief from his eyes, opening his throat and unplugging his ears.

Upon hearing those powerful and moving words, the war chief and the people wished to hear more. Ayenwatha told them of the Peacemaker and his message. All agreed the message was good, but they were still fearful.

"Will not the other nations attack us if we put down our weapons?" they asked.

"In the morning," Ayenwatha said, "the Peacemaker will join us. Look then toward the south. You will see the smoke rising from the fires of those who have heard and accepted this message."

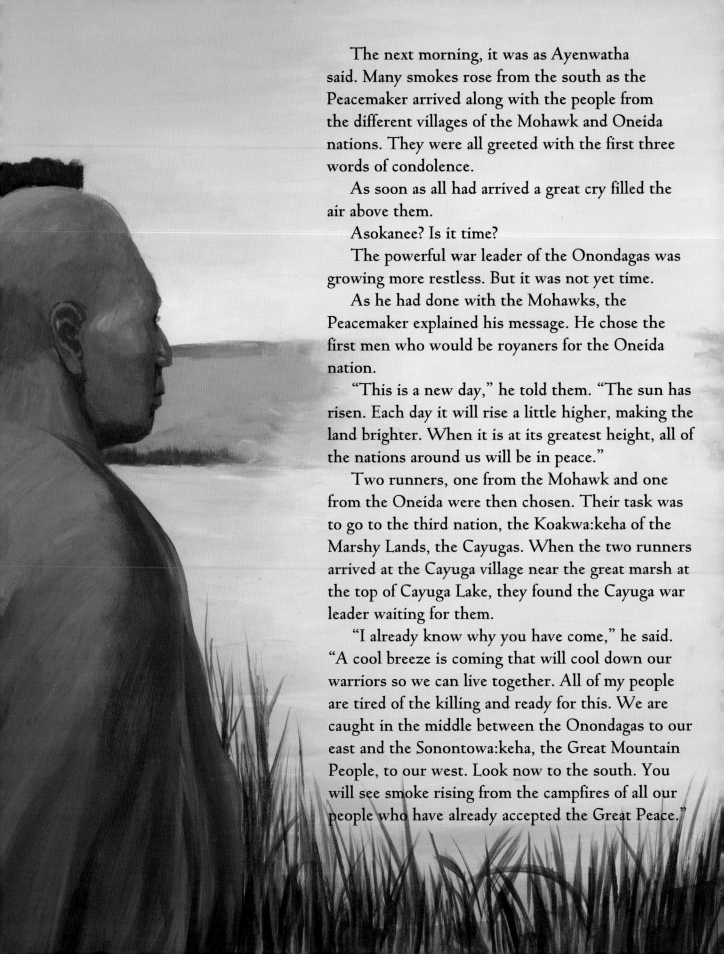

The next morning, it was as Ayenwatha said. Many smokes rose from the south as the Peacemaker arrived along with the people from the different villages of the Mohawk and Oneida nations. They were all greeted with the first three words of condolence.

As soon as all had arrived a great cry filled the air above them.

Asokanee? Is it time?

The powerful war leader of the Onondagas was growing more restless. But it was not yet time.

As he had done with the Mohawks, the Peacemaker explained his message. He chose the first men who would be royaners for the Oneida nation.

"This is a new day," he told them. "The sun has risen. Each day it will rise a little higher, making the land brighter. When it is at its greatest height, all of the nations around us will be in peace."

Two runners, one from the Mohawk and one from the Oneida were then chosen. Their task was to go to the third nation, the Koakwa:keha of the Marshy Lands, the Cayugas. When the two runners arrived at the Cayuga village near the great marsh at the top of Cayuga Lake, they found the Cayuga war leader waiting for them.

"I already know why you have come," he said. "A cool breeze is coming that will cool down our warriors so we can live together. All of my people are tired of the killing and ready for this. We are caught in the middle between the Onondagas to our east and the Sonontowa:keha, the Great Mountain People, to our west. Look now to the south. You will see smoke rising from the campfires of all our people who have already accepted the Great Peace."

The runners carried that good news back to the Peacemaker and Ayonwatha. But as soon as they finished telling them, once again the air shook with that loud cry.

Asokanee? Asokanee? Asokanee?

"The great war chief of the Onondaga is even more impatient to fight us," the Peacemaker said. "But we must wait until the Cayugas and Senecas are with us."

When the leaves had turned red, the Peacemaker and Ayonwatha proceeded with the Mohawks and Oneidas to the Cayuga villages. There the Peacemaker raised up more leaders to the role of royaners. The former head war chief was given the name of Takaheyonh, He Looks Both Ways, because he had accepted the Great Peace even before the Peacemaker got there and was waiting for his arrival.

"Now," he said, "Three nations have accepted the Great Peace. The sun is higher in the sky and its light has grown brighter."

It was time now to bring the message of peace to the Sonontowa:keha, the People of the Great Mountain, the Senecas. Of all the five nations, they were the largest and most powerful.

"Only your people have dealt with the Senecas," the Peacemaker said to the Cayuga royaners. "If we all go to their lands, they may think we are coming to fight. You, Takaheyonh will lead a delegation to them. The rest of us will wait here while you go to extend the Great Peace their way."

Takaheyonh did as the Peacemaker said. When he and his party crossed into the Seneca lands, they lit their fires by the eastern side of Seneca Lake and waited. Soon, runners from the Senecas arrived.

"We know that you Cayugas have joined with the Mohawks and Oneidas," they said. "All of our villages have been told. Our warriors are ready for battle."

Takaheyonh held out his hands. "We have come here for peace, not war. We are here to offer a new way, a way to make our people whole."

The Seneca runners were not moved by his words. "You cannot pass!" they said, shaking their bows and war clubs.

Takaheyonh was sad when he returned to tell the Peacemaker what happened. But the Peacemaker was not discouraged.

"I will go by myself," the Peacemaker said in his gentle voice. "I will try to persuade them."

Then the Peacemaker made the long walk all alone to the shore of Seneca Lake. He made his fire and waited as the smoke rose. Soon, the same runners who'd met Takaheyonh arrived.

"Why are you here?" they asked.

"I have come to stop the warfare," the Peacemaker said, his voice calm as a gentle breeze. "My message is one of peace according to the original instructions given us by the Creator."

The runners lowered their weapons. They led him back to the village where their two war chiefs waited.

"Why have you come here?" the head war chief asked.

Then, as he had done so many times before, the Peacemaker explained his mission. He told how he had brought the message of peace first to his Wendat people, then to the Senecas, Oneidas, and Cayugas.

"I am building a great longhouse," the Peacemaker said, "that will extend from east to west. All of our people will live within it as one family in peace. I wish you to join and be the keepers of the western door."

The rarontaron of that Seneca village nodded his head. "We accept your message of peace," he said. "We cannot speak for the other war chiefs west of us, but we will send runners to them." So it was that another rafter was added to the great longhouse. The Peacemaker gave the former head war chief of the Senecas

the new name of Skaniotar:io, Handsome Lake. The second war chief, who had remained on top of the great hill to watch and see if warriors were coming to attack became Shekartonias, Level Skies. "Now," the Peacemaker said, "the sun is almost at its greatest height and the day of Peace has become brighter."

As soon as those words were spoken, once again that great and threatening voice filled the sky.

Asokanee! Asokanee! Asokanee!

The Peacemaker looked back to the east. "It is almost time," he said, his voice calm. "We will all gather at the shore of Onondaga Lake and wait for Jigonhsaseh to arrive. It is only through her and the other women that peace can be kept and grow."

When they arrived at the shore of the lake, the leaders of the four nations began to talk about how they would approach the great war chief of the Onondaga. He was said to be taller than any other man. His evil magic was so great that his body had become twisted and snakes grew from his hair. There was no agreement about what to do. They began arguing so much that it seemed as if the Great Peace would end before it had fully come into being.

"No!" the Peacemaker shouted.

Everyone stopped talking and turned to him.

"We must speak with one voice," he said. "Let us create a nation where everyone listens to whoever speaks, knowing that they will have their own chance to speak in turn. We will come together with the Mohawks and Senecas

on one side of the fire and the Cayugas and Oneidas on the other side. Ideas will be passed back and forth in a formal way across the fire until everyone is in agreement. To make sure everyone is understood, we will make Mohawk our common language when we come together in council."

Those words from the Peacemaker were so wise and clear that everyone was agreed by the time Jigonhsaseh arrived. The many canoes of the four nations were ready and she took her place at the head of the women.

"Now," the Peacemaker said, with Ayenwatha by his side, "we will show the great war leader of the Onondagas, the power that comes when we join together in peace."

As they began to cross the lake, the skies grew dark.

"Asokanee!" a voice rumbled like thunder above them and great waves began to rise, threatening to overturn their canoes. But the Peacemaker simply raised his hand and the waters grew calm.

Twice more that cry of "Asokanee!" filled the sky and waves rose up. But just as before, each time this happened, the Peacemaker raised his hand and calmed the waves.

Finally they reached the other side, pulled their canoes up onto the land, and took the path that led up to the place where the war chief and his men waited to do battle.

It is said by some that their first attempt to reach the Onondaga war chief failed because he caused eagles to fly down and drop their long feathers. The men of the four nations stopped to pick those feathers up until the Peacemaker and Ayonwatha urged them on. It is also said that the Onondaga war chief then used his magic to make the earth shake, knocking everyone off their feet. But the Peacemaker and Ayonwatha would not allow the people to give up.

At last they reached the place where the Onondaga war chief sat on a great stone.

"My warriors and I are ready to fight you," the war chief growled.

That is when the Peacemaker began to sing.

"Aeee, Aeee, Aeee, Aeee,
I greet the Great Law."

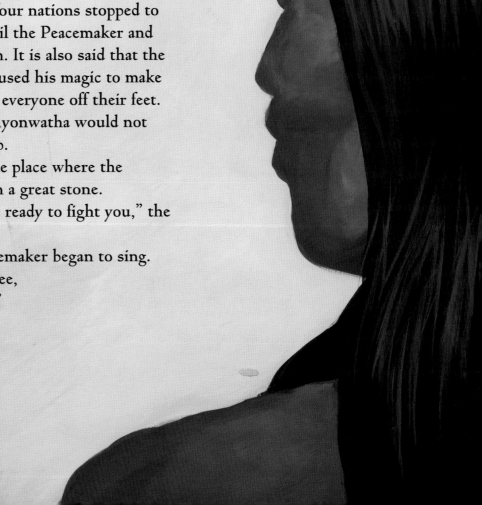

It was a song that some say the Peacemaker learned from the songs of the birds. Others say that it was Ayonwatha who heard that song first being sung by a Great Turtle as it danced. Wherever the song came from, it was so filled with peace and power that all of those with the Peacemaker joined in.

"Aeee, Aeee, Aeee, Aeee,
We greet the Great Law."

The song had such power that the Onondaga war chief and his men could not move. As the Peacemaker continued to sing, Jigonhsaseh and Ayonwatha came up to the Onondaga war chief.

"Be at peace," Ayonwatha said as Jigonhsaseh straightened the crooks in the war chief's body and they combed the snakes from his hair.

Now his mind and body were straight, cleared of all thoughts of anger and violence.

"I accept the Great Peace," he said.

"Now," the Peacemaker said to the former war chief, "No longer will you be a ruler of men. Now you will speak for them and listen always to the guidance of the women. Now our great longhouse is complete. The last rafter is in place. You will now be known as Atotarhoh, the Entangled One. All the nations will come together here at Onondaga, where you, Atotarhoh, will keep the fire that will be the central fire of our longhouse. It is here that the titles of all the royaners of all five nations will be bestowed and here that they will all meet whenever you call them together."

The Peacemaker looked around at all of the gathered people who represented every one of the Five Nations.

"Our Longhouse," he said, "will always have room for others who decide to join the Great Peace. Here at Onondaga we plant the Great White Pine. Beneath its four white roots we bury the weapons of war to be carried away by the streams that flow to the four corners of the earth. At the top of the tree we place an eagle to be our eyes and warn us of any danger approaching."

Then the Peacemaker took one arrow from each of the Five Nations and bound the arrows together. "Alone," he said, "one arrow may be easily broken. But together, like our Five Nations, they are strong. United in peace, we will be so strong that others would rather join us than take up arms against us."

So it was that the Longhouse of One Family came to be and the Great Peace was formed. The Peacemaker's message was so strong that the Great League of Five Nations

kept that Great Peace for hundreds of years until the coming of new people from across the sea brought a new time of warfare.

Yet those new people also learned from the Peacemaker's design. Such new people among the Americans as Benjamin Franklin attended meetings of the Great League and drew from it ideas that became an important part of American democracy and the documents known as the Articles of Confederacy and the Constitution. Even the eagle atop the great pine was adopted by the new nation, though it held not five arrows bound together but thirteen in its talons.

As for the Five Nations, they have not vanished. Despite three centuries of turmoil, they have kept their system of governance, their fifty royaners, the clan mothers who chose those representatives, and their longhouse at Onondaga where the meetings of the League are held and the title of Atotarhoh is still held by the Onondaga royaner who keeps the fire and calls the league together.

And they still tell this story that you've just read, not just here in America, but all around the world in the hopes that the message of the Peacemaker may still be heard, bring hope, and one sunny day be followed not just by their nations but by all humankind.

AUTHOR'S NOTE

My long relationship with Haudenosaunee or Iroquois culture stretches back to my childhood when I used to visit the "Indian Village" in Lake George, New York where Ray Tehanetorens Fadden told stories and, with his family, demonstrated traditional culture. The grandfather of David Kanietakeron Fadden, this book's illustrator, Ray founded the small but deeply important Six Nations Museum in Onchiota, New York. I renewed my acquaintance there with Ray, a true wisdom keeper, in the 1970s and frequently visited over the succeeding decades.

In 1965, while attending Syracuse University I met yet another important Haudenosaunee elder who became a friend and teacher, Alice Dewasentah Papineau, the Onondaga Eel Clan clan mother (and the sister of Chief Leon Shenandoah, who held the name of Tadadaho from 1969 till his passing in 1996). Dewasentah stopped me one day as I was coming from doing a writing workshop at the Onondaga Nation School near her house. "Here," she said. Then she handed me three things—a small lacrosse stick, an eagle feather, and an envelope with a word written on it. "This is for you. You need an Onondaga name. It's Gah-ney-goh-he-yoh. It means the Good Mind. It's because your writing must be a gift from the Creator." I accepted it. Not just as an honor, but also as a reminder to do my best to use well whatever gift with which I've been blessed.

—Joseph Bruchac

BIBLIOGRAPHY FOR FURTHER READING

Jose Barriero (ed.). *Indian Roots of American Democracy*. Ithaca, NY: Cornell University, 1988.

Darren Bonaparte. *Creation and Confederetion: The Living History of the Iroquois*. Akwesasne, NY: Wampum Chronicles, 2006.

Lewis Henry Morgan. *League of the Ho-de-no sau-nee or Iroquois*. Rochester: Sage & Brother, 1851.

Brian Rice. *The Rotinonshonni: A Traditional Iroquoian History through the Eyes of Teharonhia:wako and Sawiskera*. Syracuse, NY: Syracuse University, 2013.

Paul A.W. Wallace. *White Roots of Peace: The Iroquois Book of Life*. Sante Fe, NM: Clear Light Publishers, 1946.